Motivation

Getting Motivated, Feeling Motivated,
Staying Motivated

Justin Albert

Copyright © 2014 by Justin Albert

WHY YOU SHOULD READ THIS BOOK

Motivation provides ultimate life fulfillment. It is the driving force behind every profession, every physical action. It fuels the creation of towering skyscrapers, five-star restaurant, stellar paintings—

And yet: why is motivation so difficult to attain and maintain? Another thing: why is it so difficult to get out of bed? When did life get so out of hand?

This book analyzes these questions on both a scientific and emotional level. It lends the proper tools to build motivation in the wake of utter difficulty.

Motivation is pumping in every blood vessel, through every neuron. Human ancestors struggling to survive in the wild were fueled with this instinct: this motivation to persevere. Present people still pulse with this very intrinsic motivation. However, present-day people— because their needs are generally met, their food is generally supplied—must work for their motivation. They must keep eyes open; they must create their own understanding of their goals. Their goal is no longer: survive. Their goal is to prosper.

Procrastination. Stress. The dog needs walking, the cat needs fed. The work piles up, and motivation for desires and interests is simply out of reach. This Motivation E-book teaches the art of catching desires and interests once again and persevering. It outlines the ways one can work through the blocks in your path and attain that promotion, achieve that great legacy. One must do this: reach for real, vibrant goals in order to attain real destiny—to know self-actualization. Only with self-actualization can one feel a renewed sense of prosperity, a full sense of self.

TABLE OF CONTENTS

CHAPTER 1. MOTIVATION: THE ONLY ROAD TO GREATNESS

Humankind's all-inclusive goal is, effectively, one thing: to survive. The survival concept lurks behind all things in a person's life: behind every kitchen product, behind every home improvement store. And yet, naturally, this survival has changed over the years. It has diminished from something broad, something that must meet required caloric values and required habitat-levels into something much more refined.

What is, then, man's essential, present-day goal? To simply live. And to live well. To live better than man has before. And this goal requires innovation; it requires a push against the limits surrounding each person's life. Without breadth of motivation, people would not leave their beds; they wouldn't work to find a better life. Without motivation, people would have nothing.

Motivation is the call to action. It is the thing that pushes one from one's bed to greet the world and squeeze every ounce of energy from it. It is the thing that forces one to take one's proper stance in the world.

Do you feel, today, that you have the depth of motivation to reach your goals, to push yourself to the top of your career and become a prime person—a person with both physical and mental strength? Do you have the will to survive and the motivation to make the most of that survival?

Understand motivation and the current factors blocking you from your complete embrace of your goals. Understand the ways in which you can become the best version of yourself.

WHAT IS MOTIVATION?

Understanding the precise utilization of motivation is essential in order to prescribe everyday life goals; prescribing life goals via motivation allows for forward-motion.

DEFINITION OF MOTIVATION

Motivation, essentially, is that which initiates and maintains goal-driven mannerisms. It is an unseen force. Biological, cognitive, and social effects alter motivation; these forces mold it, form it into something that either allows growth or stagnation.

Biological effects on motivation involve the various mechanisms required at a very physical level. As aforementioned, one has kitchen appliances that rev and whir in order to maintain a very base biological motive: to boost one's caloric intake for further survival. One reaches for a glass of Coca Cola, essentially, out of motivation to quench one's thirst. These motives are incredibly basic and biological; the animals and plants of the earth have similar biological motivations, as well. A human simply has refined his reach to maintain these motivations.

Cognitive effects on motivation are incredibly complicated. Hormonal imbalances, the things one eats and the things by which one is surrounded can affect the brain, thus altering one's motivational output. Depression, stress, and low self-esteems accumulate at this cognitive level and impair judgment, thus altering continued rev for motivation.

Social effects on motivation generally involve one's environment and cultural influence. What is expected of one in one's culture generally contributes to one's sense of motivation; for example, history finds women generally staying home with children. Their motivation could not grow due to social influences. Furthermore, one's parents and one's friends alter social motivation. If one lives in a stagnant environment—an environment featuring people without conscious effort, without conscious forward-motion, one might simply assimilate into this way of life. However, if one's parents expect certain successes, social motivation might be the factor contributing to one's college graduation, for example.

THREE COMPONENTS OF MOTIVATION

1) Activation
2) Persistence
3) Intensity

Activation is the primary component: the decision to begin. A person must make this conscious decision; it is the root of all motivation. It is the very thing that allows mature motivation to grow. For example, actively enrolling in an exercise class activates the motivation to become healthy and lose weight, thus improving one's life.

Persistence is the continuation of this activation. It involves one's push through obstacles after the initial activation. It involves intense, psychological strength. For example, after one enrolls in the exercise class with the obvious intention of becoming healthy and thin, persistence must step in to truly fuel motivation. After the exercise class begins, one must invest endless hours, limitless concentration, and physicality to the point of exhaustion. It is increasingly difficult to maintain the intensity. However, if one is fueled with the proper motivation, working through the exercise class until completion garners significant strength and benefits.

Finally, intensity measures one's level of vigor after initially activating and persisting. If one persists through the various exercise classes, for example, without a significant level of concentration and exertion, one is not truly motivated. One can persist, certainly. But one will not reach the final goal of true health and strength without full-throttle intensity. Find another example in university-level classes. One can activate one's enrollment; one can attend every class; but if one does not fuel every day with study and push one's self outside of class, one will probably not achieve maximum success.

EXTRINSIC MOTIVATION VERSUS INTRINSIC MOTIVATION

Motivation is found both extrinsically and intrinsically.

Extrinsic motivation exists outside the individual. Usually, it involves the motivation to pursue exterior rewards or trophies—things resulting from successes involving other people. Therefore, extrinsic motivation involves motivation from peers; it involves impressing others via one's success. One's competitive desire can drive this extrinsic motivation completely.

Intrinsic motivation, on the other hand, exists internally. The internal gratification of completing a very personal project, for example, fuels this intrinsic motivation. Perhaps one wants to finish cleaning and decorating one's bedroom simply to feel the fresh, open understanding that one's habitat is for one's self; one's habitat reflects one's life, after all. However, if one simply wants to decorate one's room in order to impress another person, this could deem extrinsic motivation. Essentially, if one is the sole operator of one's motivation without exterior benefit, one is fueled with intrinsic motivation.

A LIFE WITHOUT MOTIVATION: WHAT HAPPENS?

What happens without that pulsing drive of motivation? Where does this lack of motivation lead? Remember that motivation is the building block for all survival, all strength in existence. Furthermore, it is the real push behind desire and interest. It is the very thing that fuels the beautiful paintings in museums, the towering skyscrapers, and the countless football games. It is human's driving force toward the meaning of life.

FEELINGS OF FAILURE AND INADEQUACY

Without motivation, one cannot move forward with one's life. One must remain stagnant. Essentially, one's hometown becomes one's only town. One's first job becomes one's only job. Lack of motivation leads nowhere.

But this lack of push does not lead to a lack of feeling. Emotion is always at play. In fact, emotion is generally the pulse behind lack of motivation. These emotions come in forms like fear of failure, fear of the unknown, incredible stresses, and low self-esteem. If one cannot work through these emotions, one cannot build a solid motivational ground. And without this ground and garnered goals, failure and inadequacy sweep into the emotional mix. One can feel a loss: like the past few years of one's life went toward nothing. One can feel a desire to do it all over again—with that drive of motivation at their backs. Unfortunately, lost years don't come back around. And inadequacy and feelings of failure linger.

Fortunately, these feelings of inadequacy can be the very reason to push toward motivation and reach toward something else. Proper use of feelings is always important. Work toward the promotion you haven't even dreamed about; wonder why you never thought to go to the gym. Understand that there's a whole world out there waiting for you. Claim it.

Chapter 2. Theories of Motivation

Psychologists' motivation analysis involves several theories. They analyze the precise reasons why one is fueled with motivation—and why one may have difficulty jumping on the motivation train.

Drive Theory

Behaviorist Clark Hull created the drive reduction theory of motivation in the 1940s and 1950s. He was one of the first scientists to attempt to understand the broad depth of human motivation.

Homeostasis: Balance and Equilibrium

Hull's theories attend to the facts of homeostasis. Homeostasis is the fact that one's body constantly works to achieve balance, equilibrium. For example, one's body finds a consistent, approximate temperature of 98.6 degrees Fahrenheit. When one dips below or above this number, one's body hustles to achieve balance once more.

Essentially, the "drive" of drive theory refers to the tension aroused by the imbalance or lack of homeostasis in one's body. In the temperature case, therefore, one's interior drive is the fact that one's temperature is out of whack. Further drives are hunger and thirst. These drives, or stimuli, force one's body into action to achieve balance in the form of a meal or a glass of water.

Therefore, Hull's drive theory acts on a sort of stimulus-response mechanism. His theory is rooted in biology and therefore takes no notice of interior, life goals. However, he does provide a decent understanding of the root of motivation.

INSTINCT THEORY

Psychologist William McDougall studied the instinct theory in relation to human motivation. His essential findings rooted the instinct theory as a way through life—a way that assured continuation of life via natural selection. Of course, the behaviors he studied were not limited to biological needs. He studied human instinct; and human instinct garners several shades of gray.

WHAT IS AN INSTINCT?

An instinct involves a tendency to behave in a specific manner without engaging in thought. The acts are spontaneous, occurring in a sort of matter of course after a particular occurrence.

Human instincts cover a broad range of occurrences rooted in both physiological and psychological needs. Physiological motivations, of course, meet hunger, thirst, and habitation needs. Psychological motivations, however, clasp something a bit more human; things like: humor, curiosity, cleanliness, fear, anger, shame, and love.

MASLOW'S HIERARCHY OF NEEDS

Abraham Maslow's humanistic theory of motivation analyzes all the basic human elements—from the simplistic biological needs to the self-actualization needs.

He breaks these needs into five stages with the idea that one's motivations can only escalate when one's needs are met at the immediate stages.

STAGE 1: PHYSIOLOGICAL NEEDS

As aforementioned, physiological needs consist of the basic, survival needs like water, food, and sleep. One must meet these physiological needs prior to building the motivation to move to the next step.

STAGE 2: SAFETY NEEDS

These safety needs involve providing one's self with proper health, income, and an actual "home."

STAGE 3: LOVE/BELONGING NEEDS

After one meets physiological needs and one has a place to live, a place in which to feel whole, one can begin to understand the benefits of social surroundings. These benefits can fall from familial ties, friendship, work groups—anything that forms a sort of relationship in which one can beat back against loneliness and find a place in society.

Stage 4: Self-Esteem Needs

One jumps to the self esteem needs stage in the convenient stage after one feels a sense of belonging. Learning that one "fits" in a society is a great link in the

Motivation

chain. Self-esteem needs allow one the motivation to achieve in one's school or work and to build one's reputation. It allows one to take responsibility of other things or other people. This is essential in the hierarchy of needs: that one does not "need" anything anymore— one is motivated, instead, to help other people meet their needs. One is further motivated to meet one's wants.

Stage 5: Self-Actualization Needs

Self-actualization involves something a bit deeper than the self-esteem stage. The self-esteem stage requires one to achieve in society, to take charge of one's self and one's life. However, the self-actualization stage motivates one to find personal growth, it motivates one to feel fulfilled by one's career, one's relationships. It might not be enough, for example, for one to simply achieve at one's job. This stage might require one to feel as if one's commitment to one's job is also making the world a better place, for example. One might do some soul-searching in this stage to truly understand one's place in the world. One cannot commit to this true soul-searching, of course, without meeting the initial four stages of the hierarchy of needs. However, to truly find one's self and truly meet one's goals, one must exist at this top stage— with all other needs completed.

Chapter 3. Depression: A Constant Shadow

Fueling one's self with the motivation to succeed; to reach one's goals is not so simple—especially with very real, human failings on the horizon.

For example, when depression rears its ugly head, one may find it difficult to remove one's self from one's bed, to eat properly, to really find rejuvenation at work.

If one finds the phrases:

"I can't" or "I don't have the energy" in one's consistent vocabulary, one might be suffering from a stage of depression. Depression affects millions of people around the world. It is a serious hormonal disorder, an interior disorder that can literally take years from one's life: take years in the way that lack of motivation can force one to forget one's surroundings, to forget one's goals.

Depression is one of the biggest contributors to loss of motivation.

Physical Exhaustion

When one is depressed, one feels physically exhausted. This exhaustion is due to low serotonin levels in one's brain. Serotonin is a general "happy" brain neurotransmitter. Therefore, it is involved with brain cell communication. It fuels your brain with excitement, with energy to get up and move around. When serotonin is lacking in your brain cells, one's energy levels drop and one's desire to enjoy one's day falters.

STAGE 1 OF HIERARCHY: PHYSIOLOGICAL

This fatigue plays into the aforementioned biological reasons for motivation. One's current, base motivation is to fuel one's self, to care for one's physical being. One must meet one's sleeping needs prior to moving on to the second stage of the hierarchy of needs. Therefore, when one is pulsing with the falters of depression, one cannot proceed to work on one's personal relationships, find proper income, or ever reach self-actualization in the form of meeting former goals. One falls back to basics. And this back to basics mechanism generally finds a depressed person back in bed.

Furthermore, standing at this basic level can occasionally find one either overeating or under-eating. Providing one's self with the proper amount of food is incredibly important. Glucose from nourishment is incredibly important for brain and muscle function. When one does not receive these glucose levels, one may fall deeper into a depressive state with less brain cell activity and thus less serotonin communication. When one over-eats, however, one feels bloated, sluggish. One may lack the motivation to proceed from one's bed due to desire to fulfill the biological requirement of digestion.

MEMORY AND INFORMATION PROBLEMS

Because tasks outside the realm of the first stage of needs seem insurmountable when one is depressed, one generally cannot keep tasks or information in one's head. One understands, at this most basic level, that one is not "up for the task." This feeling forces one to feel deep frustration; even the most simple things—remembering appointments, paying bills—can seem impossible. Memory requires the brain to communicate on a cellular level; however, the brain's activity is sluggish and malformed.   Feed a motivated feeling staying motivated feeling motivated

MOTIVATION VERSUS DEPRESSION: TAKE CHARGE

Building back motivation after a depressive episode can be difficult. One feels completely lost, rundown—incapable of even the most basic scenarios. Unfortunately, fueling one's depression by staying in bed for several days simply leads to more bed days. Depression leads to more depression without the proper fight.

However, fighting back is not impossible.

Follow these steps in order to take your life back, to bring motivation and revving energy back to your brain.

1. Force Something Good Upon Yourself: This is the idea of "opposite action." Essentially, you should force yourself to do something you do not want to do. Your brain is telling you, continually, to stay in bed. To maintain a low-level of activity. You know that watching seven hours of television will contribute to a continuation of your depression. Therefore, go outside. Go for a walk. Your behaviors can and will change your emotions in a positive way. Changing your emotions will allow

13

you to motivate yourself, push to the further steps of the hierarchy.

2. Set an Alarm and Make Your Bed: When you find yourself in the realms of depression, you will be uncertain of time restraints as you avoid everything in your life. Therefore, your alarm alerts you of a proper schedule. It tells you when you should get up for the day, when breakfast, lunch, and dinner is, and when you must run an errand. Furthermore, making your bed pushes you toward a visualization: your life does not have to be messy and scattered. You don't have to get back under the sheets. You can take control of your day.

3. Make a List of Things You Need to Do or Used to Enjoy: Simply visualizing the things you used to do or need to do written out on paper can boost your brain. Your brain cell communication will rev your memory of how good you used to feel when you completed certain tasks. Next, schedule time to do these things. Spread them out so as not to initially overwhelm yourself after so much low-time.

4. Meet with Friends and Family: You might not be ready to meet the challenges of the third hierarchy of needs; however, your friends and family can give you a boost. You're a part of their hierarchy of needs; and because their motivation allows them to reach toward the self-esteem and self-actualization spectrums, they will be able to watch out for you, to care for you better than you can care for yourself. Simply trying to reach out toward family and friends will force you to

understand the importance of relationships on your mood. Furthermore, this will take you out of our initial environment—the environment in which you maintain your depression: your bedroom, your house.

Remember this: you will not want to work through this motivation. You will want to revel in it, live with your depression forever because it will seem like the easiest path. You have the true power to work through the steps of depression in order to claim your true motivation. You have goals; you have life-affirming dreams. It's easy to forget them when you're living in a sort of hole. You can reclaim your old routine.

Chapter 4. Fear of Failure: Tripping You Up on Your Path to Motivation

One's decision to refute something, to not follow through and truly chase one's goal could be rooted in a very real, psychological problem: fear of failure. Fear of failure is staggering, able to cause immobility. It forces lack of forward motion. And this fear of failure can come in many forms. One could subconsciously undermine one's self in order to miss out on larger, greater failures. This way, one can assure one's self that failure was going to happen anyway; that there was no other way.

This is no way to live one's life.

Fear of Failure Signs

Low Self-Esteem

If one is not fueled with sufficient self-esteem, the fourth level of the motivational hierarchy, one cannot truly motivate one's self. One cannot feel sufficient in one's goal retrieval. Low self-esteem is recognized with statements like: "I'll never be good enough," or "I can't." For example, if one consistently feels that one cannot read a certain high-level book, one will never try. If one never tries to read this high-level book, however, one will never incorporate the intricate vocabulary that will allow growth and forward motion. However, this fear of failure in the form of low self-esteem allows for no motivation to read this book.

RELUCTANCE

Sheer, initial reluctance to incorporate new projects into one's schedule is a sign of fear of failure, as well. Simply trying new things is a way to recognize new goals and assimilate into ready motivation. It is a way to realize all the beauty and wonder in the surrounding world. An example of this can be found in a simple, every day decision to either go to a known restaurant or journey to a new, distinct restaurant for dinner. The known restaurant has brilliant food; this is already known. However, this restaurant is already a part of one's world. The distinct, new restaurant could be terrible; it could be wonderful. The reluctance to try, however, shows an innate fear of failure. This fear of failure translates to all aspects of life and can alter motivation to push one's boundaries.

PERFECTIONISM

If one shows a willingness to try only the activities one knows to be already successful in one's life, one might be fueled with fear of failure. Understanding that one can incorporate perfection into one's every day activities allows for no forward motion. Learning new activities and gaining experiences, instead, allows for forward motion. And this requires motivation.

SELF-SABOTAGE

Self-sabotage comes in many forms. Procrastination—putting things off until the last minute—is a form of self-sabotage. If one cannot plan ahead, work toward a

17

proper goal, one is sabotaging one's self and thus already writing one's self off as a failure. This is a sign that one fears that working toward goals will still lead to failure; if one doesn't work, one already understands the outcome of the goal.

FEAR OF FAILURE: THE DECISION TO LIVE, ANYWAY

The thing about failure is this: one can choose precisely how to look at it. Failure affects everyone. It is a consistent part of one's life.

However, if one grows to see failure as the end of one's life—if one grows into this fear of absolute failure perspective—one might regress into not living at all. After all, failure is a part of one's life for a reason: to learn. One learns from failure as much or even more as one learns from successes.

An example is found with traveling. When one journeys to a foreign city—say, Paris—one may rehearse a few general French phrases, a few words to "get by." However, it's perfectly natural not to compete at the top language level the first time you try to converse. When something is not natural, it probably leads to a few degrees of failure. But the truth behind this failure is this: one must learn and grow in order to truly push the limits of one's life.

Defeating fear of failure, however, requires a pure eyesight adjustment. It requires one to understand the lessons one is meant to learn. One might say, after several rounds of failure, that failure is the true meaning of motivation and life. Failure happens all the time; it is the root of life. However, motivation to push through and defeat failure is triumphant, allowing complete rejuvenation and a "take charge" mentality. One can completely own one's life and reach the "self-actualization" stage of one's life.

STEPS TO OVERCOME FEAR OF FAILURE

1. Set small goals for yourself. Large goals are overwhelming to anyone suffering from fear of failure. Small goals allow compartmentalization. They should push your limits; however, they shouldn't be too challenging. They should simply be stepping stones to allow you confidence boosts; these subsequent confidence boosts will allow you to look to greater, larger goals with less fear.

2. Understand what the worst-case scenario of your failure will be. Occasionally, the worst-case scenario if you fail is a complete disaster. However, most times, failure simply leads to disappointment or a bit of embarrassment. Sure, these are not fun feelings. However, feelings pass. Remember that.

3. Have a Plan B. Allow yourself to have a back up plan in case you fail. That way, you'll still have the ability to take action if your initial plan fails. You won't be left a little jarred, uncertain of your next steps. It will make you feel more confident, more sure of yourself in the initial plan.

4. Analyze every single outcome. Fear of failure is a result, often, of fear of the unknown. If you map your outcomes, write them out for visual

understanding, the fear of the unknown will retreat. You will have the ability to prepare without the large, aching blank in your brain: that fear of the unknown keeping you from valid, clear thoughts. Put your best foot forward.

Don't allow your fear of failure to affect your every day life. Take action and feel the life inside of you. Every day is a new beginning with a different, more vibrant ending. It is up to you to take each day by the reigns.

Chapter 5. Low Self-Esteem: Believing in Your Motivation

Low self-esteem: the classic battle between one and one's self. As aforementioned, self-esteem warrants the fourth level of hierarchy directly after relationships. Self-esteem is, generally, the idea that one is worth a career, worth a reputation. And having proper self-esteem allows motivation to work toward these things.

Unfortunately, low self-esteem attacks from a deep, impenetrable place. It affects one's motivation in that, of course, it does not allow full grasp of step four of the hierarchy. But furthermore, it attacks one's motivation because it forces one to have false thoughts of inadequacy. It forces one, generally, to feel as if one's goals and aspirations are unattainable. "I would never be able to do something like that," is a classic low self-esteem sentence. And thus, the low-self-esteem person thinks, why should one try?

Motivation allows goal-seeking and life-building while low self-esteem literally strangles, forces one to remain back in place. Forward growth cannot occur.

Telltale Signs of Low Self-Esteem

Watch out for these telltale low self-esteem signs. These signs warrant significant attitude adjustments. Only with proper self-esteem can one truly attain one's goals and pulse with motivation.

INDECISIVENESS

The classic indecisive person generally has low self-esteem because, essentially, that person is afraid of making a poor choice and thus seeming "wrong" or "stupid" to peers. The person freezes, assuming that his friends or family would choose a much better option. He does not trust his own opinions.

HIDING BEHIND A MASK

The low self-esteem person is generally not-all-there. Basically, this person fakes his true self, revealing a false person to his surroundings. He lives a life of secrecy, hoping other people won't sense his unrest with his own life and his own self. Therefore, this person is constantly performing. And this constant performance is a straight-way shot to anxiety.

LACK OF ASSERTION

The person who lacks assertiveness gives up incredibly easily. Essentially, this person feels that any decision or any movement they make will utterly result in failure. This person automatically believes he will be wrong; therefore, he doesn't argue his points or feature his opinions. This person will generally give up after the first defeat understanding that anything additional he tries will be a failure, as well. Furthermore, he is wishy-washy, agreeing with everyone on the surface.

PRAISE DEFLECTION

The low self-esteem person cannot take a compliment. This person will simply refute it and argue it with all the reasons he believes he does not add up. The praise could be anything; this person has enough considered, complicated reasons why he should not receive compliments. Furthermore, this person grapples with the fact that this "compliment" might not be that at all; he believes, perhaps, that this compliment is a crash of sarcasm.

INHABITING THE PAST

The low self-esteem person does not live in the present moment. Instead, he is constantly thinking about either the past or the future. He is dwelling on the past and the times he thinks he failed; he is filled with only regrets and fears for the future failures. Therefore, he cannot bother to build the proper motivation to create a better future for himself. Instead, he will continue to think that he is either not good enough for this considered future; alternately, he will continue to consider all the mistakes of his past. This forward and backward motioning allows for no growth.

MOTIVATION VERSUS LOW SELF-ESTEEM

One must work through one's low self-esteem in order to truly claim one's motivation to work forward. One must drop the staggering cling to the past and the candid fear of the future in order to motivate one's self for the present. The present is, after all, the only thing for which one has control.

RID YOURSELF OF LOW SELF-ESTEEM

1. Begin to notice your interior self-critic and stop him in his tracks. Oftentimes, if you have low self-esteem, you will reflect anything unfortunate

23

about your surroundings back on yourself. You will feel social or environmental effects that will ultimately make you feel low, like you're not good enough. For example, you might think a peer is more intelligent than you. And this thought will spiral—turn toward hatred of your own level of intelligence. Learn to stop these thoughts. Learn to understand that this thought is only going to spiral your self-hatred out of control. It is not constructive; it is simply digging you deeper.

2. Stop comparing yourself to other people. You've heard it all before, sure: everyone is unique. It's absolutely true. The things you're good at are not the things other people are good at, and vice versa. However, just because you can't bowl as well as the person a few lanes down, you are not a bad, evil, stupid person. If you'd like to become a bowler, you can work for it. Of course you can! But if you continue to compare yourself to your surroundings, you'll never be happy. There will always be someone else to compare yourself to; the constant invalidation will ultimately defeat you.

3. Respect yourself. If you don't personally respect yourself, other people will have a hard time finding the respect for you as well. Respect that you have different skills and different traits than other people. Understand that you are worth more than you think you are; you are worth that promotion, that leading role. You deserve close, intimate relationships and a fulfilling life.

4. Understand that you are the perpetrator. No one else can make you feel bad about yourself. If

someone were about to physically attack you, for example, you would do something about it. You would run away; you would fight back. You wouldn't let yourself come to bodily harm on purpose. And yet you allow yourself, every day, to hurt yourself from the inside out.

5. Surround yourself with positive people who say genuine, positive things and have good outlooks on life. Remember that so much of your motivational outlook is representative in your environment. If your environment is fueled with positivity, your outlook on your goals and yourself will be positive, as well.

6. Write good things about yourself to yourself. Keep a journal. If you feel bad or like you're not worth your goals, write a few things you know you like about yourself. Concentrate on those things. Read the things out loud to allow your brain, your mouth, your teeth to understand them. You are more than your rough interior thoughts. You are so much more.

Chapter 6. Lack of Interest: Fueling Yourself to Greatness

Another element in the train of lack of motivation lies in sheer lack of interest. This lack of interest can come in many forms; after all, one does not have interest for all things at once. However, if there is a sheer deficit of interest contributing to a lack of motivation, one's lack of interest is contributing to a lack of forward motion. If one lacks interest and enthusiasm in the great offerings of the world—in meeting people, in going places, in trying new things, or in furthering one's career—then one will lack the proper motivation to do these things. This seems natural. However, there are several contributing factors for lack of interest that subsequently lead to direct lack of motivation.

Signs and Reasons for Lack of Interest

Several factors result in a sheer lack of interest with one's surroundings. The human is an ultimate, fragile creature.

Lack of Stimuli or Incentives

A stimuli or incentive is, essentially, the thing waiting at the end of an accomplishment. It is the carrot dangling before a horse, charging the horse forward. It is that thing one deserves after completing a great task: that promotion or that smaller sized dress. If one is not fueled with a sense of accomplishment after completing something or if there's nothing waiting at the end of the tunnel, one might lack the understanding for why one should do anything.

DEPRESSION

Depression, mentioned in chapter three as an over-arching reason for lack of motivation, also sees a complete lack of interest. This, as discussed earlier, is because of the hierarchy of needs. One simply needs to feel better: to sleep, to eat, to be. Therefore, one cannot reach past this first stage to assimilate with various life interests. This comes from a decreased level of serotonin, a neurotransmitter that boosts energy and positivity. Without serotonin, positivity about any interests is lacking.

POST-TRAUMATIC STRESS DISORDER

On a more serious note, lack of interest and depression can result from post-traumatic stress disorder. PTSD develops after something traumatic occurs in one's life. This traumatic thing can be anything. However, it results in a mistrust of one's surroundings. It often forms a sort of mold or mask in order to shield one from the world. This shield ultimately results in a lack of interest. One cannot think beyond the shield or the shell of unrest one feels. One gradually dives into a "safety net" from which one cannot build the proper motivation to retrieve a sense of excitement or hope for the future. One has a very fragile psyche; one must work through several things with a licensed professional prior to taking small steps toward an initial goal to ultimately retrieve one's life once more.

LACK OF BELIEF IN ONE'S SELF

The lack of interest-laden person may simply live in a shield of his own lack of confidence. For example, if one feels that anything one does will fall short in some way; if one feels that one's "best" isn't good enough, one may resort to a hiding mechanism. One may begin to feign interest and then ultimately lose interest altogether. One's interests may only lie with things one knows will be successful. Therefore, one's life contains no true forward motion. One's life remains stagnant.

ELEVATING INTEREST IN LIFE TO FUEL MOTIVATION

STEPS TO FUEL INTEREST LEVELS

1. Re-evaluate yourself and your activities. When you actually do things, what are your reasons for doing them? What are your incentives for completing the dishes, for example? Your clean kitchen is, of course, your incentive in this equation. And what are your reasons for exercising? Staying in shape; losing weight, perhaps. If you have a lack of interest in things you know you have to do, write down the list of incentives for these activities. If you don't want to do your work, for example, understand this: if you don't do your work, you will not get paid. If you do not get paid, you cannot do fun activities, pay your rent, or eat lunch. The incentive for doing things might be a little shaded, a little gray. However, if something is worth doing, there's always an incentive. For example, doing something creative might not result in an

immediate reward. However, the feeling of creating could be your stimulus.

2. Look to the hierarchy of needs. Are your personal biological needs being met? Do you have a proper home and a proper income? Are your friendships worthwhile? If none of these things are true, your lack of interest and lack of motivation is understandable. Build the motivation to fuel yourself with the right foods, the right nutrition. Get enough sleep at night and call your loved ones. If you do this, you may begin to feel the enthusiasm for life rejuvenate.

3. Understand what matters to you. Make a list of your favorite things. These things could be anything: anything that makes your heart beat a little faster and your mind wind a little easier. Analyze how the things in your life that matter to you affect your goals. Understand what your actual goals are in relation to the things that matter to you.

4. Make private time for yourself. Soul-searching is absolutely required to rejuvenate your lack of interest. Writing lists of your favorite things, remember the things in life that truly made you feel good prior to this lack of interest will be the things that truly fuel you for the future. Build your motivation once more; picture yourself in the future as the person you'd like to be. There's no reason you cannot reach out and become him.

CHAPTER 7. PROCRASTINATION: BLASTING AWAY THE LAZINESS

Procrastination is a roadblock in the motivational road to one's goals. It involves putting off the activities that would fuel one more directly down this desired path—the path to one's assumed greater identity. The existence of procrastination seems counter-intuitive. Why would someone place unneeded burden on himself? Why would someone want to lag behind on the path to greatness?

Procrastination involves the fact that one convinces one's self that relaxation and calm fun should take the immediate place of one's required activities. Procrastination is an ugly friend; it leads to utter panic and less sufficient completion of goals. The television calls; the sun is shining. The reasons for immediate procrastination are boundless. However, the actual, hidden reasons are incredibly complex.

CAUSES OF PROCRASTINATION

COMPLEXITY AND HELPLESSNESS

Things can get tricky in the world. Jobs become complex; homework comes in all shapes and symbols and styles and languages. One looks at the work all laid-out; it looks like gibberish. It seems, at first glance, completely complex. One feels utterly helpless and without the proper intelligence to complete it. One cannot comprehend the resources one must have in order to push through. Therefore, a quick retreat from thinking about it leads to greater and greater procrastination. A five-minute break turns into a twenty-minute break; and therefore, one's motivation simply slips away.

FATIGUE

Of course, with all those tasks at hand, one cannot do anything without proper rest. Pushing through and finding the motivation to work through an assignment requires clear neurotransmitter brain action; it requires sharp and quick cell-to-cell communication. That is, your neurons must fire correctly. When you don't sleep or don't get enough water, your brain cannot translate things as efficiently. Therefore, any task that requires concentration will be a no-go when one is fatigued.

FEAR OF FAILURE

This continues to pop up as a reason for lack of motivation. The truth is, however, fear of failure is the root of several life problems. Fear of failure can cause one to put off tasks. One is always looking for the "right time" to do something—the right time when fear of failure doesn't feel so high. However, fear of failure is always a humming, gray area in one's brain. It is always lurking. Therefore, this right time to do a task and thus complete a goal never appears.

The fear of success is also a factor in procrastination. Success can be scary. It can alter the present situation; one must grow and change with it. And growth and change, of course, can be overwhelming. Putting off work and goals is incredible in that it allows one some fifteen, twenty minutes to just "be." However, both success and failure of one's tasks leads to forward motion; it leads to further life lived. While it's wonderful to "stop and smell the flowers," one must push past this procrastination in order to truly rev with motivation.

Resentment

Perhaps this category is best suited to children: children put off cleaning their room and doing their homework out of a sort of resentment. The complaints spew.

However, adults can feel this similar sense of resentment that leads to procrastination as well. The resentment is pushed to bosses, to family members, to friends. One feels resentment, for example, when one's boss assigns too much work in a short amount of time. One cannot complain outwardly; however, one can stew at a desk and glare at the computer screen for a few hours. This will, in the end, result in nothing but: ultimately finishing the assignments and moving on or, perhaps, finding another job. However, the resentment that leads to procrastination does one no favors.

Give Procrastination the Boot

Steps to Eliminate Procrastination and Fuel Motivation Once More

1. Break Your Task Down into Steps. Every task has basic, essential components. You can look at these basic components are small pieces of a greater whole and work on them piece by piece instead of confronting the whole monster at once. This way, you'll be able to outline your time a bit better. For example, if you're writing a report, think of it in sections. The introduction. The

conclusion. The chapters. Compartmentalize and do research for each chapter as you go instead of shoving all the required information into your head at once. Everything all at once is overwhelming.

2. Remember a Past Success. You've absolutely completed something successfully before. It's the only reason you've gotten this far; it's the only reason forward motion has brought you to the current task before you. Think positively. Understand that when you completed that task, you were completely focused; other things did not affect you. Try to eliminate thoughts of the outside world and focus at the task at hand—as you've done before.

3. Reward Yourself Along the Way. If you complete two of your compartmentalized tasks, for example, you're allowed to take a short break. Give yourself a designated schedule. However, if you do not work constructively during work time, do not reward yourself. Think of it as a sort of game. Furthermore, if you complete your entire task, give yourself a final incentive: a really great, end treat. If you finish a big assignment at work, for example, reward yourself with a nice dinner that evening. Remind yourself that good things come from hard work. Prior to completing the task, think of the consequences if you don't complete the task. This could be an incentive to finish.

4. Find a Way to Make Your Work Meaningful. This, of course, relates to the incentive plan. However, if your work does not mean anything to you, you

may find it difficult to complete it. Truly analyze if your work is giving you life fulfillment. If you do not have the motivation to complete your work, try to find motivation to find a different line of work. This could allow a better self-actualization plan.

5. Work Through Your Mistakes. If procrastination kicks in due to a fear of failure, remind yourself that the only way to learn is by doing. And when you do things for the first things, you will probably fail. However, remind yourself that the only thing worse than failing is not trying. When you complete your assignment, you will have a better understanding for it.

Chapter 8. Stress and Motivation: A Delicate Balance

Stress is a chemical reaction. Just that: a hormonal, chemical reaction that occurs in the body due to a perceived threat. It was such a beneficial thing for a time: when humans lived out in the open, in the midst of real threats against their survival. The hormone cortisol springs into the bloodstream, allowing rapid heart beat and quick action. Back then, humans could dart out of danger quickly and thus live to see another day. Stress was, at one time, humanity's very lifesaver.

However, stress' link to motivation is incredibly complex. For example, when motivation to complete goals and push for that next big job promotion kicks in, one should feel a bit of stress. It's natural. The stress should be subtle: just enough to get one revving, get one's heart beating and blood pumping more quickly to the brain. This fight-or-flight response, this survival response, is linked with better performance.

However, too much stress can be incredibly unproductive in terms of motivation. Chronic stress causes illness and disease; it leads to unhappy, cumbersome lives. And when one is unhappy and ill, one cannot proceed with one's forward motion. Fulfillment cannot be reached due to physiological concerns.

Of course, a myriad of things cause stress. What stresses one person might make another person chuckle.

Regardless of its source, however, stress affects everyone on both emotional and physical levels.

STRESS EFFECTS

EASY AGITATION

Quick frustration and agitation lurks in anyone who is fueled with chronic stress. This can affect everything from relationships to the ways in which one eats. For example, this quick frustration can damage a friendship—one that was necessary for the third stage of the hierarchy of needs. Furthermore, one could eat non-nutritious foods due to an agitation with the rest of the world. This leads to an improper balance in the physiological needs stage. One cannot, then, fulfill one's motivational goals while feuding with friends and not treating one's body correctly.

UPSET STOMACH AND ACHING MUSCLES

Consistent stress causes unfortunate body reactions. Stress causes the muscles to tense up without one knowing. This causes improper digestion and aching muscles. If one must stop to care for one's stomach and one's limbs, one cannot truly push forward, full-minded with one's motivation. One's body must be in working order; otherwise, it is distracting.

PESSIMISM

As a result of too much stress, pessimism and loss of positive interest can take hold. One can view the world in only a dark, negative light. A pessimistic viewpoint does not lead to a reach toward goals; it does not allow fulfillment. It simply leads to a constant cycle of disappointment.

INCREASED SUBSTANCE ABUSE

Chronic stress can lead to increased substance abuse. "I'm ready for a drink," is the consistent after-work sentence—anything to get the stress from one's mind. However, increased substance abuse leads to a decrease of inhibitions. Of course, there's always a time and a place. But if one becomes dependent on answering stress with a substance, one will falter on the motivational path. The path to the goal is straight and narrow.

WORK THROUGH STRESSORS

Limited amounts of stress are important in order to push motivation and reach the goal. However, chronic stress is unhealthy; it ultimately rejects that for which you strive. Follow these techniques in order to calm yourself after a dramatic leap toward your goals.

STEPS TO REDUCE STRESS

1. Meditate. Sit in your chair with your back completely straight. Set your feet on the floor. Think something to yourself that is ultimately positive: "I love myself," or "I can do this." Breath evenly. A few minutes of this each day can actually affect your neural pathways. It allows you to work through current and future stressors.
2. Try a heat wrap. Place it on your shoulder for about ten minutes and relax your entire body. Close your eyes and remember to breathe deeply.

Do this every day after your immediate stressors at work or at home.

3. Aromatherapy. Look to sweet smells like lavender. Light a candle and fill your home with delightful, comforting smells. These smells enact with your brain and allow your cortisol levels to finally decrease.

4. Laugh. Laughter is the best medicine in the books. If you laugh off your stress, you'll soon find yourself easing out of the tenseness you've built up in your stomach and in your muscles. Meet with a friend and kick back. It will do you a world of good.

5. Exercise. Exercise endorphins actually beat back against stress. The work is good for your heart, your brain, and your belly. Put your feet on the pavement.

6. Eat Oranges. Oranges have a wealth of vitamin C that aids in reducing cortisol. Oranges are also delicious and revving with water. You must, of course, stay hydrated by any means necessary.

Chapter 9. The Ultimate Rewards of Motivation

Motivation leads down a long road to the ultimate success. It is, essentially, the key. At the end of the road, all goals are reached Essentially, the battle between the body and the mind reaches conclusion. The mind wins. The mind is stronger; it is sure of the broad rewards of perseverance.

Think of the ultimate rewards of motivation, the ultimate successes: the promotion has finally landed. The dress size finally fits—after all those hours at the gym. The college graduation is completed. Goals are attained every day; and yet the motivation behind those goals is the real heartbeat, the real strength across the world.

Working through all the various things: the stressors, the depressors, and the procrastinating hours that affect motivation can be incredibly tricky. People fall behind, lie stagnant and still on their road to their former goals. However, pushing through and achieving provides the ultimate reward.

The successes, of course, provide excellent bars between motivational pathways. They provide excellent rewards. But the truth of the reward lies in the perseverance—in the motivational path. Success lies in the journey, not the destination.

Self-Motivation and Fulfillment

REACH FOR REWARD

The actual reward of persevering and feeling deep, engrained motivation is, of course, assurance that your motivation is strong and unencumbered. One can work with one's self-motivation and life fulfillment to achieve further goals.

Also, there lies a sense that one has a purpose in life. One has set a series of goals and achieved those goals. One has set those goals for a reason. An example: a woman has always longed to be a ballerina dancer. She finds real depth of life in the music and the movements. She works every day for hours on her routine; she understands the movements and she glides with the music, feeling its every beat. Her ultimate success, perhaps, is her performance at the end of a long string of practices. However, her real success is that her purpose has been fulfilled. She wanted to dance. She wanted to feel whole. And thus: she did.

However, when this fulfillment and sense of self reaches this successful height, it's important to take a break. Everyone requires a recharge. Everyone deserves a few days to unwind, to take the cortisol levels down a notch in one's stress-haven brain.

This break is, in a sense, a reward. However, reach for something else. Something positive fueled with good feeling. This reward will exist the next time around when perseverance toward a goal seems nearly impossible. Remember: reward strokes positive outcomes. And life is not all work, no play.

ENHANCED POSITIVITY

Positivity Leads to Greater Goals

Forward motion is continual. After initial goals are laid to rest, one must persevere toward a greater, higher field. Failure, one understands, is a part of the road. Failure has happened before, and it will happen again; mistakes pushe toward continued education and continued knowledge.

However, because one has already been fueled with motivation and pushed through the initial battle, one leads one's self with a sense of positivity—a sense that one has done this all before. Therefore, this positivity pushes to realms outside of one's goal sector.

One's positivity actually affects others as well; other people currently striding down their own path, filled with self-doubt can look to the positive person and understand: positivity is a real fuel. It is a real fire that allows prosperity in the face of so much darkness.

Because of this can-do, goal-oriented attitude, one can eliminate fear of failure. One's procrastination is at an all-time low. And one can reach forward and work toward new, prosperous dreams—all at the very top of the five-stage pyramid of hierarchy: self-actualization.

Chapter 10. Pathway to Maintaining Motivation: You Can Do It!

Motivation maintenance. It's easy to slough it off; people do it all the time. People decide not to go to the gym; they decide not to study outside of class. They decide not to go for that big promotion, after all. But what does all this sloughing accomplish? Essentially, blowing off one's goals and procrastinating leads nowhere. It provides no forward motion. It provides no self-fulfillment or self-actualization. Life purpose is lost.

Reach for the top of the pyramid of the five stages of hierarchy toward the self-actualization realm. Proceed toward goals with open arms and wide-open eyes. The world is standing in the way, sure. Work through it.

Seven Steps to Maintained Motivation

1. Set sufficient Goals

If you understand the goals you're working toward, you'll ultimately find a timeline to suit your needs. Keep a log of the goals you'd like to reach with a list of the tasks you're required to complete. Look at the log often to understand where all your hard work is going. Understand how far you've already come.

2. Create a Work Environment

The space in which you work toward your goals and rev in your motivation should be appropriate. It should reflect your sense of self while also delivering cleanliness and ability to concentrate.

3. AVOID PESSIMISTIC PEOPLE

Pessimistic friends and family in your life can often lead you to believe all the work you're doing is unimportant, that it doesn't matter. These people are probably struggling with their own goal reaching and find it upsetting that you have such a clear path of what you want. Don't allow them to bring you into their environment.

4. REWARD YOURSELF

Remember to keep a regular schedule of work and reward. If you do a sufficient amount of work in one day, for example, reward yourself with a long lunch break or a special dessert. Understanding that your work is going toward something—your success—is wonderful. However, quick little treats along the way do a lot for morale.

5. JUST SAY NO

The word "no" is liberating. While you're screaming "yes" in every way on your path toward your goal, you must proclaim a loud no to other distractions. These distractions come in the form of stress, depression, procrastination, and low self-esteem. Allow yourself to understand that if you give in to these distractions, you will fall from your motivation. You will fail to reach your goals.

6. Don't Work for Perfection

Fear of failure is one of the ultimate reasons people don't reach their goals. If you fear failure, you fear trying. If you don't try to do something, you will remain stagnant in place. This stagnation is against the human spirit; it is against the constant evolution of the world. Reaching for perfection immediately asserts this fear of failure. If you ultimately result in failure, you will absolutely learn from the failure and move on. Perfection is absolutely out of reach. Give your everything—your very everything. This will be enough.

7. Learn to Live with Stress

Stress is a part of the game. Pressure to succeed and pressure to keep moving is constantly on your mind. And therefore, stress is pumping cortisol through your bloodstream—quickening your heart and revving your brain. Remember that stress is an important part of motivation. However, learn to deal with it. Don't allow it to linger for too long. Chronic stress is dangerous. Try meditation, exercise, and going to a clear, easy space—a space away from your stressors. You will reach your goals. Breathe steady. It'll be all right.

Keep Going

Motivation is the fuel pushing you toward your ultimate goal of life fulfillment. It gives you drive; it gives you energy. Don't give up on it. Use it for all you can. Feel that wide-open feeling, that strength in your muscles when motivation is at its peak. And keep going. You can do it.

ABOUT THE AUTHOR

ABOUT JUSTIN ALBERT:

My mission with this is to be able to help inspire and change the world, one reader at a time.

I want to provide the most amazing life tools that anyone can apply into their lives. It doesn't matter whether you have hit rock bottom in your life or your life is amazing and you want to keep taking it to another level.

If you are like me, then you are probably looking to become the best version of yourself. You are likely not to settle for an okay life. You want to live an extraordinary life. Not only to be filled within but also to contribute to society.

OTHER BOOKS BY:

Personal Growth for Teens: Discover Yourself and Become Who You Want

Personal Growth and Inspiration: Achieve Greatness in Everything You Do

PERSONAL TRANSFORMATION: A PRACTICAL GUIDE TO UNLEASH YOUR TRUE POTENTIAL: ACHIEVE SELF MASTERY IN EVERY AREA OF YOUR LIFE

Free Preview:

CHAPTER 1. TAKING CONTROL

Your fulfillment in life greatly depends on your level of empowerment. It depends on your knowledge of how much of your life you can control; how much of it you believe you can take charge of.

It is helplessness that brings about the greatest frustration in a person's life. It is what breaks the human spirit. It is what causes depression.

When a person starts thinking that there is nothing he can do to change his circumstance, he becomes a victim. Sad and powerless, he becomes stuck in a downward abyss, unable to seek help; unable to move forward.

No matter what the circumstance, you must learn to develop a sense of control.

Remember that there are two types of environments – the outside environment, and the inside environment.

The outside environment is difficult to control as there are many factors that affect it. You cannot control the weather. You cannot control time. You cannot control other people. The outside environment is something, which you need to learn to accept, something which you need to learn to predict. The outside environment is sometimes beautiful, but sometimes it can also be unkind. Whatever it brings you, remember that you need to develop a sense of control.

You develop this sense of control by understanding the strength and impact of your inside environment. Your inside environment is something you can completely take charge of. Composed of your attitudes and behaviors, your inside environment is where you make your decisions and build your personality. It determines who you are, and what you decide to do.

The idea of taking charge is truly very simple, but it takes emotional maturity and effort. Making good decisions requires wisdom, and being in control requires composure, patience, optimism, confidence and self-belief.

IDENTITY

Who are you? How will you describe your identity? If you lived in a world where people are nameless, and people looked the same, how could you be identified?

Motivation

Your notion of 'self' determines your destiny. You become what you think, so never underestimate the power of your thoughts.

Pay attention to how you think, what you do, how you act and what matters to you. Think about the people you spend your time with, the tasks that take up most of your efforts. These things give you an idea of who you are and what you strive to become.

Think about your answers to the following questions:

1. Are you a leader or a follower?
2. Are you a thinker or a doer?
3. Are you generally happy or sad?
4. Are you content or unsatisfied?
5. Do you love what you do?
6. Do you feel healthy or sick?
7. Do you think you are a good or a bad person?
8. Are you especially good at anything?
9. Do you know who you want to be, or what you want to become?
10. What do you strongly believe in?
11. What are you passionate about?
12. What are the things you are certain you will never do or approve of? (Values)
13. What are things you want to do but can't?
14. What are your regrets in life?
15. What is the essence of life to you?

Your answers to these questions should give you insights about your perception of who you are. Take a brief, honest moment to examine your thoughts, and assess whether or not you are happy with your self-identity. If you say that you are happy, then you can generally stay the way you are, but keep in mind that there's always room for improvement. If you say that you are unhappy, do you know why? One thing is certain: there are things you need to change if you say that you are unhappy. And that includes your perspectives.

CONSISTENCY VS. CHANGE

There is a never-ending journey to self-discovery, and part of that journey is a battle between being consistent and being different.

There are so-called *expectations*, built-in labels and ideals about your identity, which you have learned to believe and accept. These labels may be a result of your personal history, your personal reflection, the people you are surrounded by, the experiences you consider important, and to some extent, your environment and circumstances.

Look at the answers you have given to the questions presented in the previous section. Can you come up with tags or labels that come as a result of your self-assessment? Can you determine events, experiences or reasons as to how you have answered the way you did to those questions? Identifying details such as these will help you validate your ideas, and enable you to understand how your way of thinking actually shapes your reality.

Do you ever get the idea that you are "smart" or "stupid" just because someone said so?

Your identity is influenced by the people you are surrounded with. You learn from the people you spend your time with, and become like them in some way – walk like they do, use the same words they use, watch the same shows that they watch. While group belongingness is important, do not lose your sense of self. This means that with or without your group, you should have a clear idea of who you are. Nevertheless, remember to surround yourself with positive people, and people who hold you in high regard. Be with people who know and feel that you are important.

As your notion of identity is influenced by your circumstances, and by all the other factors mentioned here previously, know that by default, *you will normally live up to expectations.*

What is sad about this is that even when these expectations are negative, there is a tendency for you to live up to them because you are hardwired to think that this is who you are, and that there is nothing you can do to change it. This is why people tend to be consistent. And when you are consistent, you become predictable, and most people are okay with that. This is because predictability comes with less stress and less conflict. It brings about the same old attitudes, routines, lifestyles and behaviors which you and everyone appear to have learned to deal with over time. Again, it feels okay because "if it ain't broke, don't fix it."

And I agree.

If you are okay with "okay," then stay there.

However, I take it that you are not satisfied with only doing *okay* – that's probably one of the reasons you are reading this book. At some point, you want to experience *change*.

Now, change can be beautiful, but only if you know what you want to change into.

Review your self-perception with the help of the guide questions presented in this chapter. Look at the labels placed upon yourself and find out which ones you want to keep and which ones you want to change. Have a clear, specific idea of who you want to be and what you want to become.

Once this is clear to you, examine your mindset. "I can change." "I can be better." "I am made to be a better individual." "I can be really great if I wanted to."

For any real change to take place, you must believe in yourself and what you can do. You must be strong and unyielding, and you must be very certain.

When you think you have no more room for change, the battle is over – you have given up, and so, you have already lost.

THE SHIFT

The "shift" or the change you are after does not happen automatically and it does not happen easily.

There are different ways to change. Most people try to change one behavior at a time, and this is very challenging. That's because the old labels still stick around and after some time, you find yourself reverting to your old habits.

The secret to a successful shift is this: change who you are -not just certain aspects of yourself. To make a successful shift, you need to redefine your identity, and become a new person.

Let's say you're "Joe," and people's expectations of you include that you are tough, insensitive and carefree. For the longest time, you have naturally lived up to these expectations. However, after careful evaluation, you realize that you are unhappy with these labels and that you want to become a new person: strong, caring and responsible. So now you redefine yourself, and in essence, you stop being a "Joe" and you become a "John." In effect, you stop smoking, you stop drinking too much alcohol and you stop partying too much. Instead, you spend more time in the office to get a promotion, you go out with your family on weekends, and you watch your diet and regularly exercise. Why? Because in your head, that is what Johns do, and you figured that you are a "John" after all.

You don't have to literally change your name to make the shift work, but you need to be strongly convinced that you are who you want to be. You have to be so strong in what you believe and know about yourself, that no matter what other people say, and what happens around you, you are still certain about your identity.

EMOTIONS

Your emotions tremendously influence your behavior. Many of life's decisions are made based on feelings, rather than logical analyses. Relationships are a perfect example. You tend to choose to be with the person who makes you *feel* loved – someone who makes you *feel* happy.

Emotions, however, need to be mastered. The same emotions which bring about love, happiness and enthusiasm can turn into hate, loneliness and indifference. The person who once decided to get married and be bound to someone for life, can be the same person who wishes to end the relationship by getting a divorce.

Knowing that your emotions have a significant role in your life means that you need to take time to keep your emotions in check. What emotions do you often feel? How do you get to feel like so?

Our emotions are based on how we interpret other people's actions towards us, as well as other circumstances such as the events that happen to us and around us. Because we do not have direct control over other people and events, we become overwhelmed with emotions when we perceive negative experiences. The key to mastering emotions is to use one's feelings to do something great. No matter how positive or negative the emotion seems to be, you need to learn to use it to find more meaning in life. You need to find a way to benefit from your positive or negative emotion.

And this is how you do it:

Motivation

1. *Know how you feel.* Don't deny your emotions. Acknowledge that they are there.

2. *Understand why you feel that way.* Sometimes, it is very easy to explain why you feel the way you do about something or someone. But sometimes it can be complicated, so use that opportunity to learn more about yourself. And once you have acknowledged a certain emotion or feeling, learn to *accept* that you feel that way.

3. *Find out what positive thing you can do with how you feel.* No matter how bad the situation is and how bad your feelings are, there are good things you can do with your life. For instance, people who have experienced violence and abuse can choose to stay feeling angry and wounded. They may even act negatively towards others, due to distrust or due to the idea of revenge. On the other hand, people who have experienced abuse may also choose to transform their feelings of anger to motivate actions that will help other people who may be vulnerable to the same situation or experience.

4. *Remember your past.* Constantly learn from your "negative" experiences, and use your "positive" experiences to establish strength and confidence.

5. *Take action.* Do something with how you feel. You can change the way you feel by what you think, say or do.

Look out for feelings of discomfort, fear, hurt, frustration disappointment, guilt, hopelessness and loneliness. These emotions are catalysts for change, so make sure that the decisions you make to create that change are well-thought and will help create a positive outcome.

Refuse to be a victim of your own negative assumptions, and instead, be capable of choosing positive interpretations to the things that happen to your life. It will not always be easy, but it is a way for you to keep moving forward. It is the way by which you can accomplish personal breakthrough.

CHAPTER 2. TAKING ACTION

When you determine an area of your life that appears to be "stagnant," you need to take action. The truth is that there is no "stationary" status. You either move up or move down – you can't stay in one place for too long. That is why you need to keep going forward.

Remember that the higher your standards are, the higher the demands of commitment to action will be needed to attain your goals.

To be committed to take action entails finding your passion; there is a huge tendency for you to perform well in something that you are passionate about, and this will serve as a motivation for you to keep on doing better.

How do you know what you are passionate about? If you are passionate about something, you normally have a lot of things to say about it. You come up with many ideas. You are immensely interested and you are excited to come up with something new or different from time to time. There may be highs and lows, but you are driven and motivated to work towards your goal because it gives you a sense of purpose, importance and empowerment. And it is your passion that will enable you to go the extra mile for your dreams, your goals, and your vision. Your passion will make you persevere, and perseverance is your ticket to long-lasting success.

ONE LAST THING

If you enjoyed this book or found it useful I'd be very grateful if you'd post a short review on Amazon. Your support really does make a difference and I read all the reviews personally so I can get your feedback and make this book even better.

Printed in Great Britain
by Amazon.co.uk, Ltd.,
Marston Gate.